P9-DGU-223

WHY SMALL

CHRISTIAN

COMMUNITIES

WORK

Msgr. Timothy O'Brien
with Margaret Gunnell

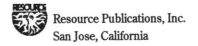
Resource Publications, Inc.
San Jose, California

Editorial director: Nick Wagner
Editor: Kenneth Guentert
Prepress Manager: Elizabeth J. Asborno

© 1996 Resource Publications, Inc. All rights reserved. No part of this
book may be photocopied or otherwise reproduced without permission
from the publisher. For reprint permission, contact:

Reprint Department
Resource Publications, Inc.
160 E. Virginia Street #290
San Jose, CA 95112-5876
408-286-8505 (voice)
408-287-8748 (fax)

Library of Congress Cataloging in Publication Data
O'Brien, Timothy, 1927-
    Why small Christian communities work / Timothy O'Brien with
    Margaret Gunnell.
        p.   cm.
    Includes bibliographical references (p.   ).
    ISBN 0-89390-371-X
    1. Basic Christian communities—United States. 2. Parishes—United
States. 3. Church renewal—United States—Catholic Church. 4. Catholic
Church—History. 5. Jesus Christ—History of doctrines. I. Gunnell,
Margaret. II. Title.
    BX2347.72.U6037   1996
    262'.26—dc20   96-7045

Printed in the United States of America

00 99 98 97 96 | 5 4 3 2 1

To the memory of Father Matthew Sullivan, whose friendship and encouragement have motivated me from my seminary days.

Contents

Acknowledgments

The Scripture quotations contained herein are from the Revised Standard Version of the Bible, copyrighted 1962, by the Division of Christian Education of the National Council of the Churches of Christ in the United States of America, and are used by permission. All rights reserved.

The quotation on pages 53-54 is reprinted from John Grindel, *Whither the U.S. Church?*, copyright 1991 Orbis Books. Used with permission. All rights reserved.

The quotation on page 36 is reprinted, with permission, from *Redemptive Intimacy: A New Perspective for the Journey to Adult Faith,* copyright 1981 by Dick Westley, published by Twenty-Third Publications, P.O. Box 180, Mystic, CT 06355. Toll free: 1-800-321-0411. Further reproduction, without permission, is prohibited.

The quotation on page 4 is reprinted from Leo R. Rock, SJ, *Making Friends with Yourself,* copyright 1990 Paulist Press. Used with permission. All rights reserved.

The quotations on pages 13 and 34-35 are reprinted from *Church: The Human Story of God* by Edward Schillebeeckx, translated by John Bowden from the Dutch *Mensen als verhall van God,* published 1989 by Uitgerverij H. Nelissen, Baarn, reprinted with corrections 1990 © Uitgerverij H. Nelissen 1989. Translation © 1990 by The Crossroad Publishing Company. Reprinted by permission of The Crossroad Publishing Co., New York.

The quotations on pages 11 and 12 are reprinted from *Consider Jesus* by Elizabeth A. Johnson, copyright © 1990 by Elizabeth A. Johnson. Reprinted by permission of The Crossroad Publishing Co., New York.

The quotation on page 43 is reprinted from M. Scott Peck, *The Road Less Travelled,* copyright © 1978 M. Scott Peck, M.D. Reprinted by permission of Simon & Schuster, Inc.

Preface

This book is my effort to answer the question a professor of systematic theology asked me when I told him of my interest in small christian communities. He simply asked, "Why?"

Why is the Small Christian Community (SCC) movement sweeping through the American church, and what are the reasons for it? What are its roots? This book seeks to explain the development of SCC's in today's church by examining today's christology and ecclesiology.

My examination focuses on the concepts "identity" and "mission." Traditionally, our theology is our understanding of Jesus' identity and mission and of the church's identity and mission. The use of the words "identity" and "mission" are not two separate concepts unrelated to each other. They are two sides of the same coin and are interdependent. Identity influences mission, and mission impacts identity. However, being aware of the distinction between them will help give us a fuller understanding and image of Jesus, church, and parish. The identity and mission of Jesus is the cornerstone of the identity and mission of church and parish.

The theological answer to the question "Why small Christian communities?" is found in our understanding of Jesus' identity and mission. SCC's allow us to live the identity and mission that we have as followers of Jesus Christ.

This writing is a product of my sabbatical year. To all who have helped me on my sabbatical journey I am grateful. I also wish to thank Margaret Gunnell, without whose motivation and skill in refining my efforts this writing would not have seen daylight.

Finally, I have included faith-sharing questions at the end of each major section. Faith sharing is the heart of the life of a small Christian community experience. Faith-sharing questions invite an experimental response and not an intellectual response. In faith sharing we listen and accept another's sharing of their personal experience of God, and this faith sharing develops a Christian community of people who are there for one another. This true experience of community enriches our own faith life and makes our community an evangelizing witness to the world. "I will dwell with them and walk among them. I will be their God and they shall be my people" (2 Cor 6:16).

JESUS

Different images of Jesus existed in the days of the infant church. Matthew, Mark, Luke, John, Paul, and the early church fathers all had their own vision of Jesus that they communicated to their constituents. Some focused on his humanity; others on his divinity.

This dichotomy continued until the Council of Chalcedon in 451, when the church declared that Jesus had two natures, one human and one divine. The council found no conflict in this hypostatic union within the person of Jesus.

Since then the church has believed in the mystery of this hypostatic union. While the debate raged, the people and church emphasized the divinity of Jesus and minimized his human character. The people in the pews and the priest from the pulpit saw Jesus as the Son of God. Devotionalism was our response to his divinity. We stressed reverence and praise. Mary was venerated because she was the Mother of God. Jesus' humanness was lost in our need for one to save us from everything, including our own humanness.

One of my earliest memories of church is my mother dragging me to church to light candles for Caesar Brombella, a neighbor who was in the hospital with blood poisoning (lockjaw, as I remember) after he cut his arm with a saw. Mom permitted me to light two candles and reminded me that candles were signs of my prayers for Caesar. Without my prayers, the candles meant nothing.

Today, we are again in a time of christological ferment. We have a pluralism of images of Jesus. We seem to be in a time of transition. The traditionalists continue to focus on the divinity of Jesus while Scripture scholars and theologians encourage us to recover his humanity. We remain one in our belief in Jesus, but how we live that belief depends on our understanding of the identity and mission of Jesus.

Most of us grew up and lived with our image of Jesus focused on his divinity. Today's christology invites us to rediscover the humanity of Jesus. The teaching of Chalcedon is being reaffirmed—Jesus is completely human *and* completely divine.

We are encouraged to focus on the public ministry of Jesus, for it is in his ministry that he reveals his own identity and mission. We are asked to look beyond the Christ of faith to the Jesus of history. What did Jesus say? What did Jesus do? What effect did he have on people, what message did he proclaim, what lifestyle did he live? And what was the movement he started?

Focusing on the humanity of Jesus is key to our exploration of these questions. The Jesuit writer Leo Rock explains:

> There are some things that are all or nothing. The humanity of Jesus is one of them. Either he was one of us or he wasn't; either we believe it or we don't. There is no room to hedge there. There is no "say when," as we do when someone is pouring coffee into a cup or putting a portion of our food on our plate. "Say when" meaning, "Tell me when you have enough." Jesus either had all of our humanity or none of it. Anything else separates us forever from what he had to teach us about being human and makes the incarnation nothing more than a cruel hoax. Anything else makes Jesus an impostor. If our faith does not totally embrace the humanity of Jesus there is no way our faith can embrace our own humanity. And, even with faith, it is difficult enough to embrace and come to terms with our own humanity. The gospels can and do speak to our human experience because they grow out of the human experience of Jesus and those who witnessed what happened (53).

The life of Jesus is traditionally divided into four parts. The first part is the period from the annunciation through his birth and childhood. The birth of Jesus was a human event, but the focus of christology has been on his divinity. Jesus is viewed as the promised Messiah who would save Israel. Scripture does not say much about this period of his life. Our faith focus is that this baby, wrapped in swaddling clothes, is the Son of God. And we are told little about his childhood.

The second part of Jesus' life is the period of his betrayal, suffering, and death. Again our focus is on the divinity of Jesus as he died for our sins—the man on the cross is our savior and redeemer.

The third period of Jesus' life focuses upon the Jesus who rose from the dead and ascended into heaven, proving he is God.

An image of Jesus drawn from any or all of these parts of his life presents Jesus as divine.

Today we are encouraged to look at a fourth aspect of Jesus' life—his public life. Here his words are as clear as his actions. He tells us who he is—identifies himself—and shares with us his mission, as he saw it. The identity and mission of Jesus as he understood it is the focal point for today's christology.

In his public life we see the humanity of Jesus working side by side with his divinity. His actions made his disciples want to make him king; his words tempted them to run away, and some did. Jesus' power made disciples of many, but his words made them nervous. His actions made them hope he would miraculously restore Israel to glory, whereas his words told them to live their human lives by loving one another. His followers loved his miracles but struggled with his teachings.

In discovering the identity and mission of Jesus as a human being, we discover our identity and mission as human beings. In living our life as God's children and in responding to everyone as our brothers and sisters, we find our identity and mission. We are truly followers of Jesus Christ, who lived and gave meaning to our humanness. This christology, focused on Jesus' public life, is the cornerstone of our ecclesiology and the foundation upon which we develop our parish life.

The christology of my early priesthood focused on the Jesus of the cross. The crucified Jesus was God my savior who redeemed me from my sinfulness. My identity was that of a sinner. Sin was everywhere and particularly in my humanness. My mission was to save my soul through living a supernatural life. I needed God's grace to save my soul and grace empowered me to overcome the temptations arising out of my humanness. Clearly my Christian identity was not found in my humanness but in my rising above my human nature and being super-natural. In those years a dualism dominated our thinking. This dualism created a vast distance between God and me. God was good and I was sinful. Only God's grace could save me. There was nothing I could do.

This thinking influenced our theology, including our ecclesiology and sacramentology. Church was to help us save our immortal soul and sacraments were the primary signs instituted by Christ to give us the grace needed for salvation.

Today's vision of church and parish flows out of our understanding of Jesus' identity and mission. In this section, we will reflect on Jesus' identity and mission.

The Identity of Jesus

F rom the way Jesus talked of God, it is obvious that he had a special experience of God as intimate, close, and compassionate. Stemming from that experience, Jesus called God "Abba".

"Abba" is the Aramaic word a child uses to address his or her father. Jesus' own personal experience of God as close and compassionate led him to a relationship with God reflected in this title full of intimacy. The name "Abba" proclaims a personal relationship between Jesus and the One he named Abba. Jesus teaches all of us to call God "Abba," encouraging us to trust God the way little children trust a loving parent. Jesus' Abba experience was the heart of his identity: God, Abba, was the passion of his life.

Several years ago I was invited by a Jewish friend to be a guest at their family Passover celebration. Before the meal the father hides a special gift for his youngest son, and my friend had done that. During the rite, he sent his son out to look for this special gift. When the youngest son found it, he came running to his father shouting, "Abba! Abba! Abba! I love you."

The Jewish people knew they were God's chosen people, but they kept God at a respectful distance because of God's kingly holiness and almighty power. In calling God "Abba" Jesus declared that power and aloofness are *not* the essence of God's identity. Rather, Jesus proclaimed that he is the child of a loving, understanding, and forgiving Father who is present to him at all times.

Jesus' use of this word "Abba" gives us, in a condensed form, the very secret of his life, the core of what he understood his real identity to be—Jesus allowed his whole life to be shaped by this vision of God as "Abba." Abba was his life project. Jesus' God is near and affirming. This child of Mary found his identity in calling God "Abba," a title that is characterized by an extraordinary warmth and intimacy.

The Gospels present Jesus to us as someone captivated by Abba. Everything in the Gospel reveals Jesus' conviction about the active presence of Abba in every moment of his life. God was known to him as Abba, and he always responded to God as an obedient son: "...not my will, but thine..." (Lk 22:42; cf. Mt 26:42); "My food is to do the will of him who sent me" (Jn 4:34); "I have come to do thy will" (Heb 10:9).

Jesus does not use "Abba" as we think of the Father in the Trinity. These dogmatic categories of Father, Son, and Holy Spirit are not found in the New Testament but were made three hundred years later at the Council of Nicea. The church's conviction about the sonship of Jesus Christ is based on the totality of his life, death, and resurrection—not simply on his calling God "Abba."

Before looking at the identity of Jesus theologically, I want to state that I believe that we find the identity of Jesus in his mission. Identity and mission are two sides of the same coin. Jesus' relationship to God as Abba was not only the foundation of his identity but also his mission. His identity and mission are not to be separated. Our identity is found in our relationship to God and our mission is to live that relationship.

Just as we know our identity in and through the significant relationships in our life, Jesus too knew his identity through his relationship with his Father, and he invited his disciples to share in that relationship. He invites us to see who God is: a loving parent.

Traditionally, the identity of Jesus has been expressed by the use of three concepts: (1) human nature, (2) divine nature, and (3) person. The understanding of each term has changed in recent times. Our modern christology encourages us to use today's understanding of human nature, divine nature, and person.

Today, psychology, anthropology, and sociology invite us to look beyond our metaphysical definition of human nature with its emphasis on being rational. The old definition highlighted that our humanness was the source of our sinfulness. We had to overcome our human desires. In our human nature we experienced our frailty, temptation, and sinfulness. Our humanness was to be lifted up to the supernatural by God's grace empowering our soul to control our human nature.

Today's scholarship, however, encourages us to see our humanness as good. The nature of humanness is found in our constant questioning, searching, and seeking as humans who thirst, hunger, and yearn to know ourselves and our world. Humans ask questions. We are a question more than an answer. Our basic questioning nature reveals three characteristics of our human nature:

1. We do not know, but we want to know; we have an infinite thirst and capacity for knowledge.

2. We are open to the infinite and yearn for the infinite; we are always in search of God.

3. Human nature is full of hope. We even hope against hope. We do not easily despair. We can always hope against the present for the future. There is in us a capacity to imagine a better tomorrow. This imaginative ability to hope reveals we have an infinite capacity for life, which ultimately can be filled only by the source of life, God.

Although we are rational animals, we are also structured toward the infinite and will only be satisfied by the infinite God. As the great St. Augustine reminds us, "You have made us for yourself, O God, and our hearts are restless until they rest in you."

Human nature is not corrupt or bad but has a capacity and thirst for the infinite. The difference between a robot and us is that the robot is an answer and we are a question. As a question we cannot be totally *grasped* for we are always in search of who we are and who God is. That search is our humanness.

One of my mother's favorite stories was about the little boy who asked his mother, "Where do we come from?" His mother answered that we were made from dust and back to dust we shall return. The boy then got his mother on her knees to look under his bed. As she peered underneath the bed, the boy said, "Look, mom, someone is going to be coming!"

Even though God is mystery, Scripture (1 Jn 4:8) proclaims God is love. Simone Weil has reminded us that God is love in the same way an emerald is green—He is love. God would not be God without being love. The nature of love is to give itself away; love is able to pour itself out; love seeks union with the other.

This is the kind of God we are talking about when we say "divine nature"—we are describing a God ready to give God's self, empty God's self, for us.

Just as today we have a clearer understanding of "divine" and "human" nature, so today our understanding of "person" has changed from the metaphysical person—the person who exists, who has being—to the psychological person. Today "person" is thought of as a center of consciousness with the freedom to relate to other persons.

This definition has an impact on our understanding of Jesus as well as of the Father and the Holy Spirit. To subscribe to the Trinity as three separate centers of consciousness and freedom related to each other is to depart from the traditional teachings of the church.

Karl Rahner has suggested dropping the word "person" and thinking of God existing in three distinct manners of subsistence: first, God as the beginning and source of all (Father); second, God as self-expressing, always going out (Son); third, God as the power of unifying love calling us back to our relationship (Holy Spirit). Thus, there is one God in three ways of self-emptying—three ways in which God relates to us.

What happens when we put together the divine nature of self-giving love and the human nature of questioning? The answer influences our spirituality (our understanding of Jesus, church, and parish), as well as how we live our lives.

Yesterday, Catholics were reminded constantly of the competition between our human sinful ways and the life God was calling us to live. "Natural" or "human" was suspect; supernatural was God's way. Today my humanness is not in competition with God but rather is made for God. As humans we are structured toward the infinite with a hunger for truth, love, and life. The nearer we come to God, the more fulfilled we are going to be as human beings. The more human we become, the more the divine lives in us. Irenaeus sums it up: The glory of God is the human being fully alive.

Jesus was united to God more than any one of us. And so, Jesus was genuinely more human, more free, and more alive, more his own person than any of us, simply because his union with God was more profound.

Since Jesus is the "nearest" to God, then, in fact, he is the most fully human and free. The incarnation does not make Jesus less human but the most fully human of us all. He is us in all things, tempted, questioning, yearning, but without sin. Karl Rahner invites us to think of God not as three persons but as the mystery of self-giving love. If we do so, it becomes possible to see Jesus existing as the Word of God in time, who in his humanness embodies the self-giving of the God of love.

Seeing Jesus in this way is central to our understanding of Jesus' identity and the impact his identity has on us as church, parish, and Christians.

> Human nature is a deep questing mystery, thirsting for the infinite. Divine nature is the incomprehensible mystery of holy love seeking to give Godself away. The two come together in the incarnation in a personal unity which enables the human nature of Jesus to flourish. In this way of reading the dogma we do not say, "Jesus is God and in addition human as well." Rather we start at the other end and say, "As this human being, Jesus is the Son of God." Precisely as the human being he is God in time. He is fully human, fully free, fully personal, and as such he is God who has self emptied into our history. At the end of this progression of thought, what is restored to our consciousness is a way of envisioning Jesus to be genuinely human at the same time the confession of his genuine divinity does not slip away (Johnson 30-31.)

Vatican II's beautiful affirmation of Jesus' humanity provides further support:

> Human nature as He assumed it was not annulled....He worked with human hands, He thought with a human mind, acted by human choice, and loved with a human heart. Born

of the Virgin Mary, He has truly been made one of us, like us in all things except sin (*Gaudium et Spes* 22).

Jesus's humanity is the cornerstone for understanding today's spirituality—the nature of church and, therefore, parish. Today's christology gives to all who accept it the following:

- a sense that each of us as humans is a gift of God filled with the potency for God

- a sense that human nature itself is moving in the direction of God

- a much more positive sense of our humanness

- a sense that every single being is also united with God and each has his or her own special dignity

If God became one of us, then human nature is gifted with God's identification with us, then human nature is gifted by the very fact that it was assumed, not absorbed, in Him each of us has been raised to a dignity beyond compare (Johnson 32; cf. *Gaudium et Spes* 22: *Redemptor Hominis* 8).

Imagine for a moment the church and parish that will exist when all Christians believe that God became one of us so we will value ourselves and each other as gifted with a tremendous dignity, our shared humanness. In 1951, Rahner asked theologians to revisit Chalcedon. The result is the full recovery of the humanity of Jesus Christ as dogma and a new appreciation of the incomparable dignity of every human being. Church and parish is everyone accepting their own dignity and the dignity of their neighbor. In that bond of love of self and neighbor, the church and parish can and will be the living people of God. Through living our relationship as "little words," the "Big Word" lives today.

The Mission
of Jesus

Scripture clearly identifies Jesus' mission as bringing about the kingdom of God. By the use of the term "kingdom," Jesus highlights the God-focus of his mission. The term expresses a relationship between God's unconditional liberating love and our human response. The kingdom of God exists when peace, justice, and love prevail among men and women who in God are at a peace with themselves and the environment.

> The Kingdom of God is the saving presence of God, active and encouraging, as it is affirmed and welcomed among men and women. The Kingdom of God is the saving presence of God offered freely and accepted by men and women. The Kingdom takes concrete form above all in justice and peaceful relationships among individuals and people in the overcoming of sickness, injustice and oppression and in the restoration to life of all that was dead or dying. The Kingdom of God is a changed new relationship (metanoia) of men and women to God, the tangible and visible side of which is a new type of liberating relationship among men and women within a reconciling community in a peaceful, natural environment. ...The Kingdom of God is a human Kingdom with the abolition of blatant contrasts between rulers and ruled (Schillebeeckx 11-12).

The core of Jesus' teaching is the kingdom, but he gives it no definition. Jesus describes the kingdom of God as being like a mustard seed planted in the ground, or yeast in bread, or a buried treasure. The kingdom is not a place, and it is not heaven—the kingdom is right now. It is the seed planted in us, the yeast giving life, and the treasure ready to be shared. The kingdom is the presence of God operating in our life. "As you did it to one of the least of these my brethren, you did it to me" (Mt 25:40). The kingdom can be *in* the church, but is *bigger* than the church.

The kingdom overcomes evil. The kingdom of God does not destroy evil, but it gives us the power to overcome it. It takes the marginalized—the poor, lame, blind, the alienated, the discriminated against, the lonely—and proclaims God's kingdom is there.

Jesus did not say, "I am the salvation of the world" or "My purpose is to die on the cross and rise from the dead." Jesus' birth, death, and resurrection proclaim that the kingdom of God is *now*: evil is overcome; the marginalized are freed.

Very simply, the kingdom of God has to be defined in terms of the life of Jesus: the sick are healed, demons expelled, the marginalized accepted, the hungry fed, the oppressed freed, and the kingdom of heaven given to the children.

The ministry, or mission, of Jesus is to proclaim the kingdom of God. For Jesus, this kingdom is not a realm or a concept or a program. The kingdom is a symbol bearing the reality to which it refers (i.e., the activity of God in our world). Through his words and actions, Jesus invites everyone to enter this symbol, to experience its transforming power, and then to inhabit the radical alternatives it proposes. In this way, we experience new ways of perceiving reality, of imagining new possibilities and living new alternatives. Through the power of this symbol, we have been put in touch with God's activity in our world.

Jesus' message is that the kingdom of God is present now. Jesus proclaims that God's unconditional love is being communicated now. God's kingdom is taking definitive shape now. It is among us as a kingdom of clemency, compassion, and reconciliation offered by our God. It is happening now, and it must be responded to now. The kingdom message gives to Jesus' preaching its note of fierce urgency and directness. *Now*, it must be *now*—at *this* moment. Jesus' mission is to alert people to what is happening: the reign of Abba is dawning; God's future is penetrating the present.

Jesus came to alert people to what is happening. Abba is now making himself present. He is transforming the human situation. He urgently calls on us to accept the invitation. We must allow it to change our values and our vision. God's presence is penetrating our present.

Jesus' actions give life to the content and meaning of the kingdom of God. His preaching and his activity, as well as his message and his ministry, are inseparable. Through table fellowship, Jesus extended to others both himself and the mystery at the heart of his life. He chose this medium to proclaim and celebrate God's all-inclusive love. Jesus accepted people as they were. In turn, they felt forgiven, reconciled, and human again. People began to see themselves and others as Jesus saw them. Jesus challenged and overturned the values of his time—and he continues to do so.

Another way the kingdom takes concrete, visible shape is through the activity of Jesus "going about doing good." His witness to the kingdom is shown in his healing, forgiving, raising the dead, and showing solidarity with the broken and the poor.

Jesus sees the injustice and proclaims the kingdom of God is where justice reigns in the heart of people. The kingdom of God exists when justice reigns in the actions of everyone. In the kingdom of God, there is no discrimination, oppression, superiority, possessions, power, outwitting one's neighbor, cheating, abusing, or robbing. Injustice has no place in this kingdom.

The kingdom of God is forgiving without being asked to forgive, loving everyone because of who they are and not because of what they have or do. The kingdom of God is hurting when another hurts. The kingdom of God happens when we—God's children— want to empty ourselves, give ourselves to those who question, hunger, and thirst. Simply, the kingdom of God happens when we permit the divine in us to dominate our relationships with everyone and when we see everyone as our brother and sister.

Some deny Jesus' mission as the establishing of the kingdom of God now because of the presence of pain, suffering, and even death in our lives. Jesus' mission clearly is not to remove poverty, sickness, injustice, or death. His mission is to rescue the poor from their sense of shame at being outcast and to restore their worth as human beings, beloved children of God.

In the Beatitudes, Jesus proclaimed that the marginalized are blest. They are members of God's kingdom and, as members of God's kingdom, they may stand proudly against a violent society. Their being marginalized is not their fault. So often they are victims. The parables and life of Jesus make clear we must be concerned for the welfare of one another.

The conclusion may well be that it is only against the background of our liminality* that we can begin to understand Jesus' proclamation of the coming of the kingdom of God and of the need for renewal of life (metanoia) as the basis for Jesus proclaiming we are God's children. When we identify ourselves as God's children, God's kingdom becomes real. In that kingdom the hurt, pain, and suffering are made endurable by our love for one another as God's children sharing a common faith journey.

Today's biblical renewal invites us to see that Jesus is a human being who proclaims God is his Abba and that we are Jesus' brothers and sisters. With Jesus as our Lord and Savior, we are committed to bringing about God's kingdom. As a human being, Jesus lived his identity as God's Son. As human beings, we live our baptismal identity of being the children of God and by living our identities as husbands, wives, brothers, sisters, neighbors, fellow workers, union members, welfare recipients, lawyers, doctors, priests. Today's christology asks us (all of us) to see church as the great sacrament of Jesus. We are this sacrament when we reflect Jesus and his kingdom values in our lives.

For Faith Sharing

1. Share your image of yourself when you were young.

2. Share your earliest images of Jesus.

3. Share your faith image of Jesus today.

---

*
  See pages 21 and 30 for more on liminality.

4. Share your faith image of yourself today.

5. Share how you experienced God as your Father and you as his child.

6. Share an experience of God's love being present to you.

7. Share your feelings about today's theological focus on the humanity of Jesus.

8. Share your experience of God's kingdom when you were young.

9. Share your experience of God's kingdom in your life today.

10. Share an experience of how you tried to bring about God's kingdom.

CHURCH

The identity and mission of the church has changed over the past two thousand years because of the theological, political, social, and cultural environment in which the church has survived over those years. These environmental factors will continue to impact the church's future.

My purpose is not to review the identity and mission of the church in all periods of history but simply to contrast the identity and mission of the disciples and the early church with the pre- and post-Vatican II church. I will then look at the factors influencing tomorrow's church.

Before we look at the changes in the identity and mission of the church, we need to understand two terms that influence the pattern of these changes. Father Eammon Bridin, in his book *Rediscovering Jesus*, suggests that the two terms "liminality" and "communitas" help us to understand the identity and mission of the church in a given period of time.

Liminality describes those situations in our life which fill us with a hunger and a thirst for a fuller life. Liminal experiences often confront our life's pattern. They challenge us.

Liminal experiences can be the result of personal sin, or they may have no guilt connection but they hurt, for example, the death of a loved one, sickness, floods and other natural disasters, accidents, being diagnosed as HIV positive, or cancer. Many times we have little or no control over our liminal experiences.

The liminal experiences of life, when honestly faced, invite us to journey inward. This puts us on the threshold of new life as we look at the meaning of our life.

For many, liminal experiences are the beginning of our journey toward and with God. To be liminal is to be in need of support and encouragement from others in order to experience some healing. By sharing, liminal people begin to relate to each other and to experience being present to one another. These meaningful relationships give hope and strength for the journey.

These "other directed" relationships of being there for one another we call "communitas." Communitas is a kind of spontaneous other-directed relationship, characteristic of people living liminally who want to grow. Communitas is not about community or structure, systems or institutions. Communitas is not about people living together or working together for a purpose. Communitas *is* about something far more important: people being there and living for each other.

In today's society, liminality and communitas are often experienced in facing addiction by being in Twelve Step programs. Drugs, alcohol, sex, abusiveness, anger, perfectionism, and many other behavior patterns invite us to experience our liminality. Conscious of our liminality, we recognize our need of others. When we walk away from our addictions and stand naked, we are liminal. As we stand on the threshold of a journey to free ourselves, we know we cannot do it alone—we need help. If you have walked the journey, be there for us. We cannot do it alone. Together, we experience our shared dependence on a higher power.

The Church
of the Disciples

The kingdom of God is the liminal situation into which Jesus invited his disciples. He called on them to cross the threshold and enter into communitas with him and with each other. There, they would experience the sustaining freedom needed for discipleship. Through communitas with Jesus, the mystery of Abba's boundless love becomes real. *They realized, for the first time, they are God's children.* They could now say, "Abba." This identity called for a complete change of heart, a total transformation, and a new life lived in response to the Abba's love. The disciples were Jesus' constant companions; they were committed to him and experienced communitas with him.

To be in communitas with Jesus is to live for the kingdom and, if necessary, die for it. To be in communitas with Jesus is to experience the Father's unconditional love of everyone. Jesus invites us to become a communitas: a people sharing a common identity and committed to being there for each other.

The mission of his disciples as they lived with their liminality in and though communitas was to go preach, teach, heal, reconcile, and baptize as Jesus did.

As followers of Jesus, his disciples were to live their lives out of service to the kingdom and with absolute confidence in the beneficence of God, with whom what seems impossible become possible.

The Early Church

The letters of Paul and the Acts of the Apostles both make clear that the early communities of Christians gathered in the homes of members, especially larger homes. Small gatherings in a home had clear precedents in both Jewish and Greek life.

In New Testament times the household was regarded as a basic political unit. The house church appears to have been the basic unit of ecclesial life up to the fourth century, when Christianity became the state religion and could function publicly.

The house church was not a piece or part of a church. It was church, even as the network of churches also was church. Paul did not say to the church of Corinth that "you are part of the Body of Christ"; rather he said, "you are the body of Christ" (1 Cor 12:27).

After the first Jewish war and the destruction of the temple in 70 CE (Common Era), Christian communities forged an institutional identity separate from Judaism. By the latter decades of the first century, house churches had become a normative way in which early communities structured their lives together. The house church was the basic unit of ecclesial life in the early centuries.

The primary mission of the early church was to bear witness to faith in Abba as revealed in Jesus Christ. The commitment to Abba's kingdom called on church members to leave loved ones and become part of a family which was resented, rejected, and persecuted by the religious, social, and political structures of the time. For many, their witness led to martyrdom.

To live their mission, the early Christians needed each other. An integral part of their mission was to support and heal one another. In the reality of the oppression they faced, they found

24

their strength in loving, affirming, and believing in one another as Jesus had loved, affirmed, and believed in his followers. This witness of their commitment and love of one another is what attracted followers. Their courage in the face of death itself, their faith in the coming of God's kingdom, their finding of their strength in their relationship is their witness—and their witness was their mission.

The Pre-Vatican II Church

This is the church in which many of us were raised. This is the church which evangelized America. This is the "edifice" church, the church of the Catholic school and health systems. This church set itself apart and strived to be the finest, the greatest, and the best.

This is the church of obedience, control over an individual's conscience, grace annihilating weakness, confession destroying guilt, distrust replacing self-confidence, individualism above community, religious being superior to laity, rank above identity, "rightness" and perfection being more important than love and relationship.

This is the church born in reaction to the reformation, weaned on the milk of self-discipline, nurtured on the bread of church over self. This is the church that evolved in response to the social, cultural, and political environment of its time. Its roots are in the Council of Trent; its flowering is in the growth of its membership and institutions. The word best describing this church is "institution." The institution was a fighter.

This church focused primarily on the divinity of Christ and, therefore, our unworthiness. This church proclaimed there are two ways of life: (1) natural, which is the source of sin, and (2) supernatural, which leads to heaven. *What was important was saving our immortal soul.*

The identity of this church was not "what God has done for me" but "what I have neglected to do for God." Sacraments were sources of God's grace, and they alone could save me. Penance, sacrifice, and the putting down of self were the preparation needed for God's grace.

The mission of yesterday's church was to save itself, prove itself, isolate itself. This church had a poor self-image, saw itself persecuted, and saw as its mission to grow strong through self-discipline. The mission of this church was to:

- have its members believe in the church, but not in themselves

- save souls by its members living in the one true holy and apostolic church

- continue handing on the power of priesthood through ordination and preserving the link to the apostles by the consecrating of bishops

- have control and order and protect its members from evil—"obey, pray, and pay" is the cliché that critics used to describe its mission

- be Mater et Magister, mother and teacher of the flock, and because of its addiction to being all things to all people, the church saw as its mission to keep its members as dependent children: Holy Mother church will provide for all you need. Good children who conform and find their values in everything the church teaches will be saved.

In many ways, the mission and the identity of this church cannot be clearly separated. The identity of this church can best be described by the words "institutional" and "hierarchical." The mission of this church could best be described as the savior of souls.

The Post-Vatican II Church

This is the church in transition, trying to discover its identity and mission in the documents of Vatican II. Its liminality was the radical change it was asked to incorporate into itself even though it had previously seen change as evil. If "institution" describes the pre-Vatican II church, "freedom" describes the church immediately after Vatican II.

"The people of God" is how Vatican II identified the church, but this church lacked conviction about its identity as the people of God. The fact was that some people were fighting Vatican II and its changes while others were taking these same changes to extremes. This was clearly demonstrated in the liturgical reform debates. Some wanted no change while others wanted change beyond what was recommended.

During this period, I was a pastor and lived with a parish in liturgical conflict. When we wanted to remodel our parish liturgical center and brought in as our consultant Mr. Bob Rambusch, a group soon opposed these changes. They called our consultant "The Music Man" who came to our parish to create problems. I will not share the names I was called. Eventually, the parish center was remolded and received awards, and the people are proud of their church today.

What did it mean to be "the people of God?" What voice did the laity have in the church? Parish councils and finance committees which advised the pastor were created in many parishes—with mixed results.

CHURCH

In these years, the church was confronted by developments in the human sciences and was forced to let go of its simple answers based on metaphysical, epistemological, and liturgical answers to all questions.

Its mission was to be ecumenical and evangelize. From a church set apart, we were called to reach out to others and stress our commonalty rather than our differences. From the black-and-white of yesterday's absolutes, the church journeyed to the land of grays and struggled to be comfortable.

This church, confused about its mission and identity, was bound to experience problems. It saw the exit of many priests and religious who shared the vision of Vatican II but became disenchanted with a church with a confused identity and mission. The grayness of the church produced an indifferent people. Mass attendance dropped from eighty-five percent to forty-five percent, where it remains today.

This church was a transitional church. It could not let go of the certitude of its yesterday and live its today in its identity of being the people of God. Like the chosen people wandering in the desert, the church yearned for the clear identity of Egypt: being slaves. It did not want to let go of its certitude. It made the nine first Fridays; prayed the rosary daily; went to confession either weekly or, at least, once a month. Life still was about saving the soul, with God's grace. To leave that security and go out into the desert with the identity of being the people of God is a hard challenge to accept. It has not been easy to let go of our yesterday, live our today, and move into our tomorrow.

In the years since Vatican II, the church has struggled to be the people of God. St. John tells us God is love, and God's nature is to empty or pour himself out. To be the people of God is to be people in love ready to pour ourselves out to bring about God's kingdom. To pour ourselves out, we must first recognize our need for each other. Accepting and living our relationship as God's children is the rock upon which church, as the people of God, is to be built.

The Evolving Church

Tomorrow's church will evolve through our continued growth in three areas:

1. expanding our understanding of our liminality

2. changing our structure in response to the social, cultural, and political environment of today

3. finding our identity and mission as church in Jesus' identity and mission

Liminality

Yesterday's liminal experience was sin—my consciously hurting God, others, or myself. Sin put me on the threshold of needing personal forgiveness. This was my liminality. I came to confession and received new life. For Catholics, it was the consciousness of our sins that kept pulling us back to God.

Today, many human experiences make us liminal and in need of God. Our own lack of self-esteem impacts our liminality. The thoughts, words, and actions of others can put us on the threshold of needing help, being liminal. Today our life experiences, including pre-birth and childhood experiences as well as genetic factors, can produce a liminal person in need of healing.

Michael Crosby, in his interesting book *The Dysfunctional Church*, writes of honor and shame as our primary experiences.

These same experiences often lead us to a liminal experience. "Shame reveals an individual's basic sense of being identified with or separated from community" (12). Our shame puts us in touch with our liminality. That experience opens us to change.

Yesterday, I experienced my liminality in my sinfulness; everything I did that was wrong was "my fault." My acts were seen as free and mine. Today, I realize that many other forces outside and within me make me liminal. Now I understand that my acts are often the product of experiences over which I have little control. For example, yesterday I confessed my act of anger; today, I know my act of anger flows out of previous experiences, such as repressed feelings of rejection. While I am responsible for my actions, I now realize that it is no longer enough to only confess my faults and need for healing. I know that other steps may be necessary. Today, healing my anger comes through therapy that gets at the root of the anger.

Another example: Yesterday, addictions were thought of as sins. We confessed to being drunk over and over and God forgave us over and over. Today, we go through the painful experience of announcing, "I am an alcoholic. I need help. I need a human experience that will enable me to deal with my addiction." Hurting experiences of rejection, alienation, discrimination, domination, abusiveness, and denial make us liminal.

In the past, my liminality put me in need of God's forgiveness. While I still need and desire the forgiveness of a loving Abba, today, the understanding of my liminality puts me in need of a community with whom I can share, and they can share with me.

Liminal existence is necessary for experiencing church. To be liminal is to live on the threshold of finding self, God, and a new world. Life is a journey marked by our need for one another. Liminality is a time of exposure to new values and living by a new vision. Through our shared liminality we begin to relate to each other in a most profound, direct, and personal way. Our mission is to create a new world: God's kingdom. This is the final chance for all of us to live differently. It can happen because we have come to know God as Abba and our relationship to God as God's children. We are brothers and sisters.

A liminal experience is necessary for change to happen. Experiencing my need for healing and for a change in my life, I experience my need to walk with people sharing my liminal experience. My liminality leads me to a community of people sharing liminality and, through our shared experience, we want to be there for each other.

Our shared liminality leads us to a relationship and the shared commitment of being there for each other on our journey through life. When our journey is a faith journey of following Jesus Christ, our relationship creates church.

"Church" is people experiencing their liminality from which flows a communitas rooted in the life and teachings of Jesus Christ. Church is liminal people finding communitas in and through Jesus proclaiming we are God's children, brothers and sisters. God lives in us. We are called to heal one another by our being there for each other. In and through communitas, we journey toward the God who loves us unconditionally, and we make God's healing and love real by our being there for each other.

The Changing Social, Cultural, and Political Environment

Today, democracy is the prevalent form of governance in the Western world. Today's church faces the challenge to democratize its governance. The people of God will be church when they have a real voice in the governance of the church.

There are those who believe the church is "a divinely willed hierarchical structure" and, therefore, allows for no democratic structure. This historical misunderstanding is the cause of many disputes. As a church, we must change or we will fail to have a meaningful dialogue with today's world. Monarchies and oligarchies are anathema. To use the power of church to control is repulsive. True leadership motivates rather than controls. Only in acknowledging that our present structure grew out of yesterday's history are we free to adapt it to today's history.

Vatican II opened the windows to the process of change. The council prayerfully struggled with and extensively discussed the issue of identity and mission as well as its relationship to other Christian and non-Christian religions.

In Chapter II of the *Dogmatic Constitution on the Church*, the church is said to be all those who in faith look toward Jesus—the author of salvation—and the principle of unity and peace. God has gathered these people together and established them as the church that they may be for each and every one the visible sacrament of God's saving unity.

Another change made by Vatican II because of the changing ecumenical environment was to proclaim that the task of the church is to be holy, one, universal, and apostolic through constantly renewing herself in response to the Holy Spirit.

The Vatican II Council defined the church as the people called together by God. In the church, all believers are equal, living in the Spirit, free, children of God. All are responsible for the church as *Christi Fidelis*. God's ongoing revelation of himself in the church community is a grace, but a grace through and in the structure of historical experience. To forget this is to split the church into two parts—heaven and earth—divided by a wide, deep chasm.

By contrast, Vatican II says that the earthly church and the church endowed with heavenly realities are not to be thought of as two separate realities. Grace is not a gift from heaven; rather, grace is the presence of God in our world. Heaven and earth are not two separate realities; spiritual life and daily life do not differ. There is only one reality. It is capable of being looked at in different ways, but it is only one reality.

To separate a grace experience from a human experience is to create two realities. This opens the door to two levels in the church: spiritual and human. Then, we possess two lives: one spiritual, one human. Human sciences help us understand and cope with human life, but the church helps us live our spiritual life. This return to a dualism, a separation of grace and human experience, had led to the fundamentalism which is spreading everywhere, even in the Catholic church.

Today's challenge begins with understanding the meaning and role of authority in the church. The only real and final authority in the church is the Word of God. Authority is neither in the proclaimer nor in the listener. Authority is in the word or truth spoken—the Word of God. As important as the listening is to give life to the words spoken, and as important as the position of the proclaimer may be, the Word of God is *the* source of authority. The foundation of authority in the church as the people of God and the authority of its ministers is the same, the Spirit of Jesus Christ and the Father.

Although authority and leadership were given to Jesus' followers, there was no hierarchy among them. Today, the argument persists that pope and bishops have their authority from God, yet Scripture says nothing about hierarchy. Jesus does not exclude, *a priori*, a democratic form of government. The only argument for today's structure is "Why change it after twenty centuries?"

The reason for change is that the world is changing, and the church in its identity is the people. The people's involvement in governance is democracy, which focuses on human rights and freedom. Since Vatican II, the church itself has condemned the denial of human rights and freedom in countries governed by a dictatorial, monarchical, or oligarchical government. Democracy has a number of forms, and the church must determine what form can best serve the Word of God and the rights as well as freedom of the members. Leadership is necessary in a democracy; that leadership needs authority, but the leadership cannot appeal to the Holy Spirit to sanction decisions. The Holy Spirit is God's presence as God lives in-and-through God's people.

Today's challenge for tomorrow's church is to:

- *free* itself to be the people of God not only as a title, but as a reality

- *risk* letting the Holy Spirit live and guide the church through a democratic process involving the people

- *preserve* the leadership of hierarchy and theologians in the church

As Edward Schillebeeckx states:

> The church only has a future to the degree in which it is a saving presence in the future of human beings and their world, above all where men and women are tortured individually or as a society. The church only has a future to the degree to which it lets go of all supernaturalism and

> dualism and thus on the one hand does not reduce salvation
> to a purely spiritual kingdom or a simply heavenly future, and
> on the other hand does not become introverted and
> concentrate on itself as church, but turns outside and directs
> itself to others, men and women in the world. And in that
> case it will not think exclusively of its own self preservation
> as a spiritual power in the world (234).

The church must change to be the people of God committed to bringing about the kingdom of God here and now. The world in which we live is the world to which the church must relate. The Spirit of God is alive, calling us to be God's people by ridding ourselves of supernaturalism and hierarchical structure and opening ourselves to being committed to bringing God's kingdom here by our living as God's children, brothers and sisters of a loving Father.

Finding Our Identity and Mission As Church in the Identity and Mission of Jesus

Jesus is the cornerstone upon which church is built. The identity and mission of this church cannot be different from that of Jesus.

If Jesus found his identity and mission in his relationship to God as Abba, then we, as church, must find our identity and mission in the faith relationship Abba offers us as his children. The key to understanding this lies in fully understanding that it is a *faith* relationship. Abba calls us to be Abba's children. The relationship is not the result of belonging to a religion. Rather, the relationship is the product of our faith in a God who, in-and-through Jesus, helps us to comprehend that God is in us, with us, and among us at all times. We are never abandoned.

Faith is what joins God and us in the intimate relationship God always offers us. As Christians, we are called first to be people of faith. In my own experience, I rejoice to find many Catholics who, although legally excommunicated for being married outside the church and thus denied the practice of their religion, refuse to let their faith be denied them.

By faith, we overcome our fears and commit ourselves to God's dream for this world: that one day it will be the kingdom of all people living out a faith relationship with Abba.

Dick Westley, in his book *Redemptive Intimacy*, gives us a clear understanding of the teaching of Jesus when he points out that:

> After being with Jesus for years, Philip walked up to Jesus one day and asked, "Lord, when are you going to show us the Father?" And Jesus said, "Philip, you are looking at him. The Father and I are one."
>
> But in saying that, Jesus was revealing not only who he was, but also who we are. For Jesus was saying to Philip that God is not to be found outside of humankind, but within, in the intimacy and togetherness of human and divine promised and foretold in God's covenant with Abraham, then effected and realized in the Lord Jesus, and present in each one of us when we truly walk with him in faith.
>
> So God is human, not only in Jesus Christ, but is human in each one of us and was human from the beginning. Only no one would believe him when he tried to reveal it. With the coming of Jesus, we know definitely where God is, He is where he has always been, with, among and in his people. That is the Good news of the Gospel and the implementation of that truth is what Scripture calls the Reign of God or the coming of the Kingdom.
>
> We believe that he who fashioned us abides in us, walks, suffers and dreams with us. He is the faithful one who never abandons us. He is our Father (82-83).

In another section, Westley quotes St. Athanasius: "God became man so that man might become divine (*Re Incarnation Verti*)" (104); "Jesus is our Savior/Redeemer because he is the complete embodiment of the absolute intimacy of God and all of humanity" (117).

For Faith Sharing

1. Share a liminal experience in your life.

2. Share an experience of community in your life.

3. Share the journey you have traveled in search of the identity and mission of church.

4. Share your experience of the Vatican II church.

5. Share a liminal experience that led you to a deeper faith relationship with God and with your brothers and sisters in the Lord.

6. Share when and how you experienced church as a faith community, the people of God.

PARISH

B efore sharing an image of parish, I want to look at four human experiences integral to an understanding of parish. They are

1. vision

2. change

3. self-esteem

4. relationship

Our appreciation of these terms is important to our understanding of today's parish.

Vision

The importance of a parish's vision cannot be overstated. Our vision of parish determines how we live parish. Vision is the way we look at reality, including the world, people, ourselves, God, and church.

There is a uniqueness and individuality to each parish's vision. We see it reflected in the lifestyle of the parish.

Our parish life is dictated by our vision. Our decisions about what a parish does and does not do flows from our vision. Our vision is the foundation on which we build parish life. From our parish vision flow our plans, our programs, our liturgy, our education, and our human services. Many of a parish's problems and frustrations are rooted in its vision. How parishioners relate to one another and how they experience themselves as church is a function of the parish's vision.

Jesus came to give us a new vision of life, which is the foundation of the church's vision. The challenge of each succeeding generation has been to articulate Jesus' vision as that generation understands it. This understanding is expressed in the christology and ecclesiology of each generation. Developments in Scripture and human sciences challenge us to constantly renew our vision of parish so it is in accord with *our* generation's christology and ecclesiology.

Every parish has a vision that directs its life. In recent years, many have left their "home" parishes and gone shopping for a parish with a vision that meshes with their own. Today, our theology is changing, and among these changes is a call for a *new* vision of parish.

Change

To change a parish's vision requires a conversion among its people. Change means giving up the old vision for a new vision. This conversion begins not through teaching but through an experience that challenges our old vision of parish. Then we are ready to make the journey of learning how this experience can be an ongoing part of our life. This journey is learning the theology and the method for making the experience real in our life.

In the Gospel, Jesus brings about change through offering the people a new experience. In experiencing Jesus, people were attracted to follow him. Later, some drifted away when they realized the real change he was asking of them.

Change begins with an experience, not will-power. An infant develops an ability to love by being loved. Addictions are overcome through support groups. Experience is our greatest teacher. The experiences of our lives have been the primary parish. For change to happen, it must begin in an experience and then be fortified through education.

Change in a parish does not come easily. The journey of change happens when we begin to realize our vision is not meeting our need. It is not enough to superimpose a new vision. We must be prepared to meet people where they are and gently lead them forward.

If the primary vision of the parishioners is that parish is the source of salvation by giving grace which in turn saves them, our challenge is to help them look at what Jesus called us to do to bring about God's reign. We must carefully open their minds to Jesus' teachings about his vision and mission. They must see how Jesus invites us to find our identity and mission in his.

For parishioners whose vision is built on Mary, I invite them to remember that Mary's response to the angel Gabriel—Mary's "yes"—was to an intimate relationship with God. Her life was to be a constant "yes" to God's presence in her life, even when her own son suffered at the hands of others.

Mary invites each of us to say "yes" to an intimate relationship with God. Our challenge is to keep saying "yes" and live this intimate relationship. William Westley, in his book *Redemptive Intimacy*, reminds us that in this relationship is our salvation. Mary calls us to find salvation not in gaining grace but in living our lives in an intimate relationship with her son, his Father, and our Father.

When parishioners begin to accept that the security of yesterday was not as secure as they perceived, we invite them to, as the apostles did, get into the boat with Jesus and go out into the water where the wind and the waves fill us with insecurity. When we cry out to God, we open ourselves to a new vision.

An awareness of our liminality opens us to the possibility, and even the desire, for change in our lives. To deny, cover over, ignore, or pretend our liminality is not real is to close ourselves to change. In contrast, it is our hurts, fears, resentments, and anxieties that motivate us to seek change in our lives. Our liminality motivates us to change.

Self-Esteem

Jesus taught us to love God and our neighbors as we love ourselves. This unconditional love and acceptance of self seems to be the hardest task we face in our lifetime. In refusing to accept our real selves, we create a false self and become less human.

Total self-love and self-acceptance are the only foundation for happiness. Without total self-love and acceptance of ourselves, we are doomed to create *false* selves and limited visions.

Scott has defined self-love "as the will to extend myself for the sake of nurturing my own and another's spiritual growth" (87). This definition sees love as an act of the will. This means that love is a decision. I can choose to love myself no matter what the past has been and no matter how I feel about myself. Our choice is to love ourselves for who we are, not for what we do or fail to do. Admittedly, that is easy to say and hard to do. So often our human and religious experiences have filled us with feelings of being flawed and defective and not lovable. This experience destroys our self-esteem. To heal our feelings of being flawed, I have to begin accepting myself unconditionally. If I begin to love myself unconditionally, I will accept myself and permit others to love me just as I am.

The work of love is the work of listening to yourself by monitoring your feelings, needs, and relationships. If you love yourself, you are prepared to delay gratification and to experience something more conducive to your growth. If you love yourself, assertiveness will replace aggressiveness. If you love yourself, you will be free of codependency, an addiction to being in control. To love God and others is impossible if you can't love yourself. To love yourself opens you to a God inviting you to an intimate relationship. If you love yourself, your vision of your relationship to God frees you to make the changes your vision calls forth.

Relationship

Our individual life story begins not with the self in isolation but with the self in relationship.

I am a "we" before I am an "I."

As I grow, I begin to realize there is an "I" and a "you." That consciousness brings me face to face with the greatest challenge in living human life: to live with my own identity through living my life in relationship with others. A delicate balance in the I-we relationship is needed to live a full life.

I come into the world with a very limited capacity to love. The development of my capacity to love happens not on a mountain top but through the relationships in my life. To be the person I want to be, I need relationships. Affirmation is needed for me to be human and emotionally sound. That need exists in all of us.

In his life, Jesus affirms and is affirmed. To recognize my need of affirmation is to recognize my need of others. We all need to know we are loved. In risking ourselves to be loved, we develop the capacity to love. To love me, I must open myself to being loved by others. In being loved, I am capable of loving.

Our daily life is lived in-and-through relationships. Meet a person whose relationships are positive and you will know a content human being. Our greatest hunger is for meaningful relationships. Parents and children want a loving relationship. Husband and wife become one to live a committed relationship. Our relationships are the source of our self-esteem. To experience people loving me fills me with a good self-love. Apart from life, food, shelter, clothing, and air, our greatest need is relationship.

The quality of our relationships is the measure of our Christian authenticity. Our ability to relate to groups as well as individuals is the key to communicating the Gospel in this or any age.

Jesus' teachings can be reduced to two words: "Live relationships." Nothing is more important than the relationships in your life. Love God, love your neighbor, love yourself.

The Identity
of Today's Parish

Our vision of life, including parish life, flows out of our self-image and the self-images of the people of God in the parish. If we see ourselves as the people of God, our self-images give life to our relationships. Our parish life becomes a celebration of who we are. Our good self-image motivates us to strengthen our relationships by sharing ourselves with one another. A poor self-image makes it impossible for us to share ourselves.

Into this human reality entered Jesus, proclaiming God is our Father and we are his beloved children. In our humanness, we are the beloved of God, and God lives in us. This is not a supernatural identity or an identity we achieve through our good acts. Like Jesus, we are God's children from the moment of our conception.

Our human liminal experience can tempt us, as Jesus was tempted, to deny our identity. The devil tempted Jesus, and Jesus' experiences of rejection, betrayal, and denial led him to pray to his Father, "Not my will but thine be done." Unfortunately, too many times we go further and deny our identity. Jesus' strength and power was in living his identity completely. In good and bad times, Jesus lived his life conscious of his relationship with his Father. In living this identity as the Son of his Father, and in living his relationship to us as our brother, Jesus offers us a vision of parish centered on our identity with our Father and our relationships with one another. The purpose of parish is to help us experience and live our relationship to our Father and to one another.

Vatican II documents speak of the church as the people of God, but seven times it refers to the church as the fundamental sacrament of Christ. This identity calls the parish a sacrament.

The parish is to be a people who are a sacrament of what God has done for the world in Jesus. To discover God in nature, people, and the events of life prepares us to accept God as Jesus' Father, and our parish is to be an experience of our Christian identity in Jesus.

Celebrating our identity is necessary in all phases of our life. Birthdays, anniversaries, and family gatherings are celebrations of our identity and our meaningful relationships. Sex is a celebration of couple's committed love relationship. And parish is people celebrating and living the identity they have in Jesus.

This vision of parish asks us to let go of the dualism that makes parish a place where we go to get God's grace so that we will be saved. The busy parish of recent years is challenged by today's christology and ecclesiology to make certain that everything the parish does is to enrich our identity as the people of God. Today's theology asks us why we do what we do at the parish. Are we doing it in response to our Father's love for us? Are we doing it out of our identity as God's children?

The identity of today's parish is in our being the people of God and in our living and celebrating as God's beloved children. That experience encourages us to love ourselves and one another as Abba loves us all.

When this vision of the people of God takes hold of its people, the parish has the roots to experience itself as a community. Community exists when our identity motivates us to live in our relationship to others. This vision of parish invites us to see parish as a community of people committed to living their identity in-and-through their relationship to one another.

This vision of parish invites the parishioners to *change* how they are parish. The changes ask us to open ourselves to an experience of community. Only in the experience of being loved by people are we free to believe in a God who loves us unconditionally.

It is not my purpose to describe in detail the various experiences that can open people to change their vision of parish. I can share that, in my own life, Cursillo has proven to be a weekend in which God's love is experienced in the self-emptying love of the team and the Cursillo community. When you come down from the mountain (literally, in my community), you are radiant with the joy of having been with brothers and sisters who love you and love one another. Living today's christology and ecclesiology begins with a moving experience of God's love in the love of our brothers and sisters. Some may not need this experience, but it makes the change process easier.

After experiencing myself being loved, I want to experience a church that is ready to help me nourish a good self-image. Experiencing myself as loved, I am ready to share myself with others. I feel good about God, myself, and my brothers and sisters. In the sharing of our experiences of finding God in the ordinary events of life, we journey together into a deeper appreciation of our identity as God's children.

The challenge for today's parish is to provide its parishioners an opportunity to experience the sharing of their faith story with one another. This is today's essential experience of church.

As blood brothers and sisters keep alive their identity and relationship by sharing remembrances of their parents and their childhood, we, as children of God, live our identity by sharing remembrances of how Abba has shared himself with us in Jesus.

As human beings, our feelings are uniquely ours. Our feelings have no morality. Relationships are developed and deepened by people who can share their feelings and accept one another's feelings. Our sensitivity and openness to the sharing of feelings is the beginning of meaningful relationships.

Our christology reminds us that Jesus' identity was founded in his relationship with his Father. Jesus shared his feelings with his Father. His prayer was his sharing. Scripture points out that Jesus found time to share his human feelings with his Father. That sharing intensified their relationship. Jesus' identity and our identity are found in our relationship with our common Father.

That relationship is experienced in our sharing ourselves with one another. In the sharing of how we experience God's presence in our life, we intensify our bond with God and one another. In the living of our identity as the people of God and by sharing our experiences of our Father, his presence, love, compassion, mercy, and encouragement, we become a community, a parish.

In the same way that the identity of Jesus was experienced in-and-through his relationship with his Father, the identity of parish is experienced in-and-through our faith sharing. Faith sharing makes real our identity as brothers and sisters in the Lord. Our faith sharing results in a bonding which strengthens us to live our identity. Through experiencing our Father's affirmation, we live in the joy of being the people, the children, of God.

After the conversion experience, the parish needs to offer us a beginning experience of faith sharing. This experience invites us to find church not in our attendance and participation but in the experience of our shared identity.

Several programs offer a method for developing our skills in sharing. RENEW is the most popular. Genesis II and Free to Be Me have proven to be positive helps. The focus in these programs is on small groups gathering weekly, or every two weeks, to share Scripture and then share thoughts and feelings relating to assigned topics. Small groups give everyone an opportunity to participate. In these small groups, we listen and accept each person's sharing. We are journeying together. We need each person's sharing. Our goal is to share and accept one another. In learning to listen and in growing in our ability to share our feelings, we begin to live as the children of God

After the conversion and initiation stages, we are ready for the ongoing experience of living our identity as the children of God by our participation in the life, celebration, and sharing of a Small Christian Community (SCC).

My purpose is not to describe in detail this process. Others have done it with great clarity (e.g., Father Patrick Brennan in *Re-Imaging the Parish*; Father Art Baranowski in *Creating Small Faith Communities*; Father Thomas Kleissler, Margo A. LeBert, and Mary C. McGuinness in *Small Christian Communities*; Richard Currier and Francis Gram in *Forming A Small Christian Community*).

In the parish where I live as a senior priest, we are blessed with 150 parishioners gathering in fifteen SCCs. I wrote the following vision statement for our SCCs:

> To assist our fifteen SCCs at St. Mary's, I invite us to see
> ourselves on a journey toward the vision Jesus gives us and

Vatican II confirms. Our vision directs that journey. God
gave Moses a vision of the promised land. That vision guided
the forty-year journey of the Chosen People.

Vatican II gave us a vision of our being the people of God.
This vision was drawn from Jesus' vision of God being our
Father and we being his children. In Chapter 17 of St. John's
Gospel, Jesus shares the journey our vision calls us to walk. I
pray that they may be one—as you and I are one.

This oneness finds its roots in our being the children, the
people, of God. Yesterday's vision was of a distant God
bestowing forgiveness, grace, and personal salvation. Today's
vision is of an intimate, loving Father calling us his children
and inviting us to journey toward the oneness for which Jesus
prayed. Today, in South America and Africa, and now in
Europe and America, many have found that journey to
oneness in small Christian communities.

The journey is eight to twelve of God's people who share
this vision gathering in a home to walk a two-step process. In
step one, we share what has happened since we last met, and
our feeling response to these events. The journey is our
growing in our ability to share. As we experience the
non-judgmental response of our SCC, we move from the
sharing of events to the sharing of our doubts, hurts, feelings,
and fears. As this journey progresses, we bring to our SCC
the difficult problems and the decisions we face from time to
time. This first step leads us to experience our SCC as people
who will always be there for us.

In the second step, we grow in our oneness through the
Sunday Scripture readings touching an experience from our
life of God's presence which we share with our SCC. In the
beginning, our sharing is directed at what we think the
Scripture means. Slowly, our being there for one another
allows Jesus to touch our life and draw forth an experience
which in the sharing creates the oneness of Jesus' prayer.
This oneness is our communion. When we accept the Lord in
the lived experiences of our brothers and sisters, we have
received communion, our oneness with the Lord.

To live as the people of God is our vision and the SCC is
our journey to our being the living people of God.

The christology and ecclesiology I have shared invites us to have a vision of our parish's identity as a community of SCCs because the SCC offers an effective process for us to experience our self-esteem as God's beloved and true relationship with one another as brothers and sisters. This vision challenges us to change why and how we are parish.

We as parish are to live the intimate relationship God offers us by our faith-sharing SCCs. The SCC's identity is found in being:

- a journey and a process in which I experience myself as the beloved, chosen and precious child of God;

- a process built around our willingness to share ourselves and, thus, open ourselves to our identity and relationship;

- a process of finding our identity and relationship through our Scripture dialogue and through reflecting and sharing our lived experiences (i.e., by God's Word we are freed to make the changes the Holy Word asks of us. We read the Scriptures not to learn but to help us dialogue with God through our sharing with one another.);

- a growth process, a way of life that happens in-and-through dialogue;

- a process by which through faith sharing in a community of eight to twelve people we achieve communion;

- a process that offers a time for greeting and sharing what is happening in our lives, a time for Scripture and faith sharing dialogue, a time for shared prayer, a time for socializing and thanking each other for sharing in the dialogue.

The Mission
of Today's Parish

T he mission of Jesus, the church, and the
parish is the same: to proclaim and to enable the reign of God to
become a reality in this world. This mission has a two-fold
dimension: one of evangelization and the other of liberation.

Evangelization is welcoming all people into oneness in Christ.
We are to offer everyone an experience of his or her identity as a
child of God, as being our brothers or sisters. This dimension of
our mission calls for us to reach out and invite everyone into the
community of the people of God.

With the second dimension—liberation—our mission as church
or parish calls us to seek freedom for all people from everything
that keeps them from totally surrendering themselves to God. The
mission is to liberate people from the liminal situations that bind
them and then empower them with the true freedom they have as
the children of God.

For this mission to be accomplished, the people of God must be
committed to confronting and healing the liminality of our human
situation. This includes not only our personal sinfulness but also
the structures and systems (social, political, and economic) that
hold people back from achieving and experiencing their identity as
the children of God.

The mission of the parish is to pre-evangelize and evangelize by
confronting the social, political, and cultural issues of our day. The
parish stands neither above nor apart from the world. The people
of God are in the world and live with a number of identities and

missions. They are single and married, husband and wife, mommy and daddy, boss and worker, citizen and alien, etc. All these identities and missions are lived in-and- through relationships. What gives us the courage to live our many identities and missions is the identity and mission we have as the people of God.

History teaches that the church reflects the cultural, social, and political values of its environment. In his recent book, *Whither the U.S. Church*, John A. Grindel, CM, sees three core American attitudes impacting the identity and mission of today's Catholics:

1. choosiness or superiority

2. worldly success and wealth

3. individualism

These three attitudes influence the minds and hearts of American Catholics. Jesus asks us to live our relationship to one another without feelings of superiority over others. Jesus emphasizes our need for one another rather than for success; Jesus makes clear that our sense of community, of being God's children, is more important than a sense of individualism. The conflict between Americans and Jesus' core attitudes helps us to understand our liminalities.

Knowing who I am compels me to ask what is my purpose. In knowing his identity, Jesus was free to live his mission. His identity and mission were one but looked at from different perspectives. Who I am helps me to know my mission, and knowing my mission guides me to live my identity. There can be no conflict between my identity and mission.

> I would propose the following regarding the mission of the church in the United States. As an instrument of the reign of God in history the United States is to be an instrument in seeking the liberation of the poor on a global level through a two-fold process of empowerment of the poor and the transformation of the systems that oppress. The "poor on a global level" are especially the poor and oppressed in the under developed countries of Latin America, Africa and Asia. Liberation means primarily political and economic liberation, that is, liberation from the systems, the structures that

oppress. In so far as possible, this mission of the church
should provide the focus of all aspects of the life of the
church in the United States, both internally and externally
(Grindel 179).

The mission of Jesus and the church is the mission of the
parish. The parish's mission is to work with the larger church in
freeing the poor and oppressed so they may be able to behold
their identity as God's children and our brothers and sisters.

To believe in God involves entering into solidarity with the
weak, the poor, the powerless. This is difficult because we would
rather practice charity toward the weak, poor, and powerless than
be in solidarity with them. Remember, Jesus saved us not by
practicing charity toward us but by becoming one of us, by
entering into solidarity with us and suffering with us so as to
empower us to be able to take responsibility for ourselves and our
brothers and sisters. Today we, as believers, are called to become
vulnerable and to enter into solidarity with the weak, the poor, and
the powerless as Jesus did in his public life.

To believe in the God of Jesus is to accept a God committed to
people. His commitment demands that we be present to our
brothers and sisters. This presence to one another is the heart of
social justice. "'Lord, when did we see thee hungry and feed thee,
or thirsty and give thee drink? And when did we see thee a
stranger and welcome thee, or naked and clothe thee? And when
did we see thee sick or in prison and visit thee?' And the King will
answer them: 'Truly, I say to you, as you did it to one of the least of
these my brethren, you did it to me'" (Mt 25:37-40).

The SCC helps to bring about God's Kingdom because it:

- is a sign to the world that Christ is alive today and
  that his healing spirit is at work in the world;

- involves an inclusive love that accepts everyone as
  our brother and sister; an SCC can never be an
  exclusive group; its sharing opens it to be there for
  everyone;

- seeks to bring everyone to Jesus, in whom all of us
  are invited to experience ourselves as the beloved
  child of God;

- invites everyone to experience themselves as the espoused of God;

- helps us to keep saying "yes" to our being the beloved children of God by experiencing the love and unity in the SCC; others are attracted;

- gives to the world an experience of the unity it lives so that others can "see how those Christians love one another;"

- is a sign of God's presence, love and healing—a real invitation to a positive experience of church;

- is bound by love, which makes it a prophet to the kingdom of God;

- continues Jesus' healing ministry by offering healing to one another and to everyone by its patience, kindness, forbearance, hopefulness, and willingness to rejoice with the truth;

- makes real this healing presence of God in the world by putting itself at the service of others;

- brings healing as the members share their fears, anxieties, and hurts with one another and then experience God's healing touch in their brothers and sisters offering them the experience of their being the beloved of God;

- demonstrates the limitless healing power of God because the SCC brings the presence of God effectively into human history in a specific time, place, and situation.

For Faith Sharing

1. Share a faith change in your life.

2. Share your journey of growing in self-esteem.

3. Share a faith relationship that gives meaning to your life today.

4. Share your experience of the identity and mission of the parishes where you have lived.

5. Share your vision of the identity and mission of today's parish.

Conclusion

Believing we are God's children and that we share in the priesthood of Jesus Christ through our baptism allows us to envision the parish as the people of God. Accepting my identity as God's child and accepting you as my brothers and sisters fill me with a desire to live and celebrate our relationship. We are not strangers. We are brothers and sisters.

The church is the people of God, but who are the people of God? Everyone is God's child. Thus, the people of God are those who acknowledge their identity and want to live this relationship. By acknowledging our identity in baptism and living this relationship in church, we proclaim our identity and mission.

The challenge for today's parish is to let go of the old security blanket of individual salvation and begin taking the risks needed to know ourselves as the children of God and to live our daily life out of this identity.

"Church" is not a means to an end but a lived reality. Revelation is on-going in the lived experiences of people in community. God spoke, and today God speaks in the on-going story of people's lives. People of faith gather in community to discern the movement of God in their individual and communal lives.

A necessary ingredient to following Jesus is a consciousness of our own liminality. The people who came to Jesus were the liminal people of his day. Their hurt put them on the threshold. (Note how in your own life a liminal experience empowers you to turn to Jesus.) In the pains and sufferings of life, we reach out to Jesus. In Jesus' time, it was the hurting and sick who sought him out. When I feel all-powerful and capable of handling my life, I will not reach out to the Lord. From simple aches and pains to loneliness, divorce, neglect, and resentment, I hurt. This awareness of my liminality fills me with a need. Yesterday's answer was: Give your liminality to the Lord so he can take care of it. Today's answer is: Discover who you are in the Lord, strengthen this identity by faith sharing with a community, and you will be able to live with your liminality.

Your identity, enriched through faith sharing, not only strengthens your spiritual life but also helps you to focus on the reality of daily life by your consciousness of how God is breaking into your life and all of history.

My vision of some of the changes being asked of today's parish are the following:

- Teach, proclaim, and shout from the roof tops: We are God's children! We are good and not evil. Our Father believes in us, loves us, and never leaves us. Our Father's commitment to always be our Father frees us to believe, love, and forgive ourselves. Our Father's absolute commitment to his children, especially in our liminality, frees us never to give up on ourselves. This change of focus from my own identity as a sinner to my positive identity as a child of God calls for a basic attitudinal change in the people of the parish. Without an attitudinal change by the clergy and people, all structural changes will fail.

- The celebration of our identity as the children of God does not happen simply by participating in the lived memorial of Jesus' life, death, and resurrection (i.e., the Eucharist). To make our participation in Christ's paschal mystery a real sharing, a giving of ourselves to Abba and Abba to us, we must first share with one another in small groups.

Many of us recall that at one time our only obligation was to attend Mass. Vatican II and the liturgical renewal of the past twenty-five years asked us to participate in the Eucharist. Today's christology invites us to make the Eucharist a shared experience. The Eucharist is Abba sharing with us through our remembering, celebrating, and believing in Abba's son, Jesus. Our response to Abba's sharing is our sharing ourselves with God through sharing with one another.

- To be open to others' sharing of *themselves* is not easy. To be able to listen to their words, to understand what they are trying to communicate, and to be sensitive to the feelings being communicated is a life-long challenge. My ability to share myself, to communicate in words my honest thoughts and feelings, is influenced by my ability to be open to the sharing of others. In the experience of others accepting me as I am, by their sharing of themselves, I am freed to accept myself and then I am free to share myself. God shared in becoming completely human, being as human as you and I. In Jesus, God accepted the liminality of our humanness. God shared thoughts and feelings in the inspired messages of Holy Scripture. God shares presence in nature and in every person we experience. Finally, God shares with us in the sacraments. The Eucharist is God sharing with us. God constantly is giving and sharing.

How open am I to the ideas and feelings God shares in the words of Holy Scripture? How open am I to God's presence in the sharing of my brothers and sisters?

The challenge for today's parish is to provide parishioners with a faith-sharing experience. This experience invites the parishioners:

- to share their thoughts and feelings with one another about what God is sharing with us in Holy Scripture. Through the people's sharing, they grow in their appreciation of God's sharing.

- to share the word of God, which in turn frees us to share our own lives. In the sharing of my life with my brothers and sisters, I free myself to share myself with God. In my openness to my brothers and sisters sharing themselves with me, I open myself to a beloved God sharing with me.

CONCLUSION

To experience God as my Abba, myself as Abba's child, and you as my brothers and sisters, there must be a sharing experience. In our parents sharing themselves with us and in their encouraging us to share ourselves with them, we learned what the relationship between parent and children is all about.

Our parents sacrificed themselves so that we, their children, might experience our relationship as brothers and sisters. Today, our relationship with our blood sisters and brothers is influenced by our ability to share and accept the thoughts, words, actions, and feelings of one another. My failure to share myself with my sisters and brothers will limit their openness to share themselves with me.

In closing, I believe today's understanding of Jesus encourages us to provide parishioners with experiences of their identity by creating small faith-sharing experiences. Parish is then a community of small communities—eight to twelve parishioners gathering in a home to share their personal experience of God's sharing in next Sunday's Gospel. The basic attitude is that, as followers of Christ, we are to share ourselves with one another as God shares with us. In sharing our liminality, with its joys and its sorrows, its fears and its promises, its doubts and its hopes, we are better prepared for our sharing—together in God's great sharing, the Eucharist.

Resources

Christology

Bridin, Eammon. *Rediscovering Jesus.* Mystic, Connecticut: Twenty-Third, 1986.

Brown, Raymond E. *An Introduction to New Testament Christology.* Mahwah, New Jersey: Paulist, 1994.

Johnson, Elizabeth A. *Consider Jesus.* New York: Crossroad, 1990.

Lyons, Edna. *Jesus: Self-Portrait by God.* Blackrock County, Dublin, Ireland: Columba, 1994.

Ecclesiology

Crosby, Michael H. *The Dysfunctional Church.* Notre Dame, Indiana: Ave Maria, 1991.

Gaudium et Spes (Pastoral Constitution on the Church in the Modern World). In *The Documents of Vatican II,* edited by Walter M. Abbot, SJ. New York: Guild Press, 1966.

Grindel, John. *Whither the U.S. Church.* Maryknoll, New York: Orbis, 1991.

Rock, Leo R., SJ. *Making Friends with Yourself.* Mahwah, New Jersey: Paulist, 1990.

Schillebeeckx, Edward. *Church: The Human Story of God.* New York: Crossroad, 1990.

Westley, Dick. *Redemptive Intimacy: A New Perspective for the Journey to Adult Faith.* Mystic, Connecticut: Twenty-Third (P.O. Box 180, ZIP 06355; toll free: 1-800-321-0411).

The Parish

Baranowski, Arthur R. *Creating Small Faith Communities*. Cincinnati: St. Anthony Messenger, 1988.

Brennan, Patrick J. *The Evangelizing Parish*. Allen, Texas: Tabor, 1987.

———. *The Reconciling Parish*. Allen, Texas: Tabor, 1980.

———. *Re-Imaging the Parish*. New York: Crossroad, 1990.

Currier, Richard, and Francis Gram. *Forming a Small Christian Community*. Mystic, Connecticut: Twenty-Third, 1992.

Dolan, Jay P., R. Scott Appleby, Patricia Byrns, and Debra Campbell. *Transforming Parish Ministry*. New York: Crossroad, 1989.

Kleissler, Thomas A.; Margo A. LeBert; Mary C. McGuiness. *Small Christian Communities*. Mahwah, New Jersey: Paulist, 1991.

Mancy, Thomas. *Basic Communities*. Minneapolis: Winston Seabury, 1984.

Westley, Dick. *Good Things Happen: Experiencing Community in Small Groups*. Mystic, Connecticut: Twenty-Third (P.O. Box 180, ZIP 06355; toll free 1-800-321-0411).

Whitehead, Evelyn Eaton, and James D. Whitehead. *Community of Faith*. Minneapolis: Winston Seabury, 1982.

General

Peck, M. Scott. *The Road Less Travelled*. New York: Simon & Schuster, 1978.